#1 JOKING OFF...

What do you get when you sleep with a judge?
  Honorable discharge!

* * *

What are boobs on a Girl Scout?
  Brownie points!

* * *

Why is it so great to be a test-tube baby?
  Because you get a womb with a view!

* * *

Why did God create man?
  Because you can't teach an electric vibrator to mow the lawn!

* * *

What did the leper say to the prostitute?
  I left you the tip!

* * *

What do you have when there are one hundred rabbits standing in a row and they are all hopping backward?
  A receding hareline.

* * *

A word to the weird is sufficient!

#1
JOKING OFF

Johnny Lyons

PaperJacks LTD.

TORONTO   NEW YORK

AN ORIGINAL

PaperJacks

#1 JOKING OFF

PaperJacks LTD.

330 STEELCASE RD. E., MARKHAM, ONT. L3R 2M1
210 FIFTH AVE., NEW YORK, N.Y. 10010

PaperJacks edition published June 1987

ISBN 0-7701-0618-8
Printed in the USA

This book is dedicated to all the people who love jokes, particularly to my many friends, business associates and acquaintances who have generously shared their jokes with me over the years.

These include:

Harold, Foul Al, Alexander and Ted A., Lamar C., C.C.G., Costas K., Sandy L., Albert M., Raul N., Richmond R., Lazaris Z., the Postman, the Cab Drivers of the City of New York, the Bartenders of the World, and especially Tony the U.P.S. man, and a very special thanks to Vincent C., and to Clare, because without her none of this would have happened.

TABLE OF CONTENTS

Part One

SEX, DRUGS & ROCK 'N' ROLL

Peter and Albert are going hunting. Albert says to Peter, "I'll send my dog out to see if there are any ducks in the pond. If there aren't any ducks out there, I'm not going hunting." Sure enough, he sends the dog out to the pond. The dog comes back and barks twice. Albert says, "Well, I'm not going to go out. He only saw two ducks out there." Peter says, "You're going to take the dog's barks for the truth!" Peter doesn't believe it, so he goes to look for himself. When he gets back, he says, "I don't believe it — where did you get that dog? There really are only two ducks out there!" Albert says, "Well, I got him from the breeder up the road. If you want, you can get one from him too." So Peter goes to the breeder and says he wants a dog like the one his friend Albert has. The breeder obliges; Peter brings the dog home and tells it to go out and look for ducks. Minutes later the dog returns with a stick in its mouth and starts humping Peter's leg. Peter, outraged, takes the dog back to the breeder and says, "This dog is a fraud. I want my money back!" The breeder asks Peter what the dog did. So Peter tells him that when he sent the dog out to look for ducks, it came back with a stick in its mouth and started humping his leg. The breeder says, "Peter, all he was trying to tell you was, there are more fucking ducks out there than you can shake a stick at!"

* * *

There are two guys in a bar, and one man bets the other $10 that he can lick his right eye. The guy thinks to himself, his tongue can't be that long, and accepts the bet. The man takes out a glass eye from its socket, licks it, puts it back in and wins the bet. Then the man says, "Okay, double or nothing. I bet you I can bite my left eye!" So the guy thinks, well, he can't have two glass eyes, and says, "Okay it's a bet." The man takes his false teeth out, puts the teeth around his left eye, bites it, and wins the bet. So the winner leaves for a few minutes and then comes back. He tells the loser, "Let me give you a chance to win your money back, plus some. I'll bet you $100 that I can pee in this shot glass, which you'll put on the floor, and not miss a drop." The guy says, "Mmmm." He thinks about it very carefully and decides that there is no way the man can win this one. So he says, "Okay, it's a bet." Well, the man pees all over the bar, all over the guy, and virtually all over everywhere except the shot glass. The man says, "Okay, you won the bet! Are you happy?" The winner smiles happily.

The man says, "Great, because I just bet those two guys over there $100 each that I could piss all over you and make you smile!"

* * *

A mother has three daughters, and they are all going out on Saturday night dates. The first guy shows up and says, "Hi, I'm Freddy, I'm here for Betty, is she ready?" The mother says, "Betty, it's Freddy, are you ready?" The daughter comes down, and they leave. The next guy comes and says, "Hi, I'm Joe, I'm here for Flo, is she ready for the show?" The mother says, "Flo, it's Joe, are you ready for the show?" Flo comes down, and they leave. The third guy comes and says to the mother, "Hi, I'm Chuck ..."

And the mother slams the door in his face!

* * *

Author's note. For this joke you need a long-necked beer bottle as a prop! Stroke the beer bottle gently from top to bottom, and begin to tell the joke as follows:

This girl was telling her date about an old boy-friend of hers and while describing him she stroked a beer bottle up and down many times. Her date finally said, while she was stroking the beer bottle, "You're always thinking about him; how about thinking about me?" The girl said okay and proceeded to stroke only the top two inches of the bottle!

* * *

General Dreedle was a very meticulous man, always impeccably dressed. But one day his fly was open, and his assistant, Ms. Smith, tried to inform him of it by saying, "Sir, your barracks door is open." And he said, "What!" And she said, "Sir, your barracks door is open!" And he said, "What!" She then yelled out, "Sir, your fly is open," and he became very embarrassed. So he asked her, "When you noticed that my barracks door was open, did you also notice that the soldier was standing at attention?" Ms. Smith said, "No, sir, I just noticed a disabled veteran lying on two duffel bags!"

* * *

A boy and his father are walking along in the park, and the boy sees two dogs mating. The boy asks his father, "What are those dogs doing?" The father tells the boy that the dogs are making puppies. Later that evening the son walks into his parents' bedroom to discover that they are making love, and the son asks the father what they are doing. The father says, "We're making you a baby brother." The boy says to his father, "Turn Mommy over, Dad. I'd rather have a puppy!"

* * *

This girl was talking with her girlfriends and told them that she calls her boyfriend Rolling Rock because he likes to drink beer whenever they make love. The second girl said, "I call my boyfriend Seven-Up because he has seven inches and it's always up." The third girl said, "Well, I call my boyfriend Jack Daniel's because he's a hard licker!"

* * *

What's the difference between a sorority girl and a bowling ball?

You can't get more than three fingers in a bowling ball!

They say that kissing spreads germs.
I spend a lot of healthy evenings!

* * *

The world's greatest lover:
This man was having sex with a woman ar
first thing she said was, "Are you in?" And
they had sex she said, "Were you in?"

* * *

Love is the triumph of imagination
intelligence!

* * *

He held her close against him, a warm
satisfaction covering them both.
"Am I the first man you ever made love
asked.
She studied him
said. "Your face

L
sh
w

your fat ass?" The woman says, "No, he didn't
out you."

* * *

etes have athlete's foot, what do astronauts

ile toe!

* * *

you get when you cross a stud and a debtor?
one who's always into you for at least ten

* * *

those oldies but goodies.
rthur was off on a hunting trip, so he asked
of something to protect
men in the court.
a hole in it and
hat good
magic

What do you call a man who's afraid to have oral sex with his wife?

Chicken of the sea!

* * *

A sailor walks into a bar with a wooden leg, hook hand and an eye patch over his eye. The bartender says, "What happened to you?" The sailor says, "Well, a whale bit off my leg, and I was in a sword fight and lost my hand, and I went out on the bridge and a bird shit in me eye."

The bartender says, "Well, how could you lose your eye if a bird shit in it?"

The sailor says, "It's easy when you've only had a hook for a week!"

* * *

What do you get when you sleep with a judge?

Honorable discharge!

* * *

What is a condominium?

A prophylactic for midgets!

* * *

What are boobs on a Girl Scout?

Brownie points!

* * *

There are three presidents on a sinking ship.

Truman says, "Save the women!"

Nixon says, "Fuck the women!"

Kennedy says, "Do we have time to fuck the women?"

A man wakes up one morning, and when he looks in the mirror, he sees a strange growth on his forehead that looks for all the world like a tiny penis. Panicked, the man runs to the doctor and, sure enough, the doctor confirms his worst fears. There is, in fact, a cock growing out of his forehead. However, the doctor tells the man not to be concerned, that when the penis reaches full size, he should be able to remove it with no problem. "Oh, my God, no," wails the man. "I couldn't stand staring at that thing until it stops growing." "Oh, don't worry," counsels the doctor. "You won't see it. The balls will cover your eyes."

* * *

How do you recognize the most attractive man in a nudist colony?

He's carrying two glasses and twelve doughnuts.

* * *

What do a wildcat and a condom have in common?

You don't want to fuck with either of them!

* * *

Popular Sayings

There's a party in my pants, and you're all invited to come!

* * *

Wine me, dine me and 69 me!

* * *

I hate to advocate drugs, violence and insanity, but they've always worked for me!

No one can have a higher opinion of him than
I have. . . .And I think he is a dirty little beast!

* * *

What do you give to the man who has everything?
  Penicillin!

* * *

A relay is the second time around.

* * *

A bachelor is a man who prefers to ball without
the chain.

* * *

Orgasm: the gland finale.

* * *

What do you call a truckload of vibrators?
  Toys for twats!

* * *

Then there was the man who had the horrible
deformity of five penises attached to his scrotum.
Not that he let it bother him. In fact, during a physical
examination when the doctor asked him how he managed to get his pants on, the man replied that there
was no problem. His pants fit like a glove.

* * *

A psychiatrist was taking a tour of an insane asy-
lum to inspect the facility's rehabilitation program
and was quite pleased with what he saw. In the first
room he visited an inmate who was dribbling a basketball around the room and shooting baskets with

amazing skill. When questioned, the inmate proudly stated that he had great hopes for the future, and when he was released he was going to become a great basketball star. In the next room the psychiatrist found a man hitting a baseball that came at him from a pitching machine. And again the patient seemed very happy and hopeful, stating he intended to become a baseball player when he was released. However, when inspecting the third room, the psychiatrist was puzzled. The only thing he found was a patient humping a large sack of pecans. When he asked the inmate what he was doing, the patient looked up and replied, "I'm fucking nuts, man. I ain't never getting out of here."

* * *

What is better than four roses on a piano?
  Two lips on an organ!

* * *

Why do elephants have four feet?
  Because eight inches isn't enough!

* * *

How do you get a shopping-bag lady pregnant?
  Come in her shoes, and let the flies do the rest!

* * *

Have you heard about the new Procter and Gamble product?
  Toxic shock absorbers!

* * *

Have you heard about the new Toxic Shock rock group?
  They only play ragtime!

What do eating pussy and the Mafia have in common?
One slip of the tongue and you're in deep shit!

* * *

How can you tell a head nurse?
The one with dirty knees!

* * *

Moving along a dimly lighted street, a man was suddenly approached by a stranger who had appeared out of the shadows nearby.

"Please, sir," asked the stranger, "would you be so kind as to help a poor fellow who is hungry and out of work? All I have in the world is this gun!"

* * *

How do you keep a moron in suspense?
Say nothing!

* * *

How does a Frenchman hold his liquor?
By the ears!

* * *

A donkey and a lion are lost in the desert. The lion says to the donkey, "I'm very horny. I want to fuck you." The donkey says, "Okay, as long as I can fuck you back." The lion fucks the donkey, comes and dismounts. The donkey says, "Okay, it's my turn." The donkey is fucking the lion and says, "Turn around, I want to kiss you."

The lion says, "If I could turn around, I'd eat you."

What do you get when you cross a rooster and a peanut-butter sandwich?

A cock that sticks to the roof of your mouth!

* * *

An office manager had a money problem and he had to fire an employee, either Jack or Jill. He thought he'd fire the employee that came to work late the next morning. Well, both employees came to work very early. Then the manager thought he'd catch the first one to take a coffee break. Unfortunately, the employees never took a coffee break. Then the manager decided he'd look to see who took the longest lunch break. Strangely enough, neither Jill nor Jack took a lunch break; they both ate their sandwiches at work. Then the manager thought he'd wait and see who would leave work the earliest, and both employees stayed after closing. Jill finally went to the coat rack and the manager went up to her and said, "Jill, I've got a terrible problem. I don't know whether to lay you or Jack off." Jill said, "You'd better jack off, because I'm catching a bus."

* * *

What's six inches long, two inches wide, has a head on it and women love it?

Money.

* * *

An old man went to a bar, picked up a beautiful woman and took her home. The next day a small drip appeared on the head of his penis, so he immediately went to the doctor. He told the doctor of his encounter, and the doctor examined his penis.

The drip was obvious, and the doctor said, "Sir, do you know where this woman lives?" The man said, "Yes!" The doctor said, "Well, you better get right over there. I think you are about to come!"

* * *

An elderly couple were driving down the highway, headed south, and a policeman pulled them over for speeding. The officer walked up and said, "Roll down your window!" The old lady said to the man, "What did he say?" The old man said, "He pulled us over." The old lady said, "What did he say?" The officer said, "Lady, your husband was speeding." The lady said, "What did he say?" The man said, "He said I was speeding." The officer said, "Where are you coming from?" The man said, "We're headed south from Pennsylvania." The officer said, "I remember Pennsylvania. I got laid there once, but the woman was terrible at sex." The lady said to her husband, "What did he say?" The man said, "I think he knows you!"

* * *

Did you hear about the infertile woman?
    She couldn't bear children!

* * *

What do a weatherman and a sexually aroused woman have in common?
    They are both interested in how many inches, and how long it will last!

* * *

I opened up a lingerie shop and became king of the underworld overnight!

My wife's interested in clothes.
Too bad she's not interesting in them!

* * *

His clothes are in a clash by themselves!

* * *

This policeman is sitting alongside a road, and all of a sudden he sees a truck loaded with a hundred penguins approaching him. He pulls the truck over and says, "Why don't you take these penguins to the zoo?" And the man driving the truck says, "Okay." A week later the policeman is in the same spot, and the same load of penguins comes by, but they're all wearing sunglasses. So the cop pulls the guy over and says, "I thought I told you to take these penguins to the zoo?" And the man says, "I did take them to the zoo." And the cop says, "Well, what are you doing with them now?" And the man says, "I'm taking them to the beach!"

* * *

Do you know the new bra called the "Bird-dog"?
It makes pointers out of setters!

* * *

A five-year-old little girl runs into the house and says, "Mommy, Mommy, can I get pregnant?" The mother replies, "Of course you can't, dear!" The little girl says, "Mommy, Mommy, are you sure?" "Of course I'm sure," the mother says. The little girl runs out to the backyard and says, "Okay fellas, same game!"

Little Johnny got a chemistry set for his birthday. He was down in the basement, mixing chemicals together. His father came down to see how he was doing, and Johnny appeared to be hammering a nail into the wall. When the father asked Johnny why he was hammering a nail into the wall, Johnny replied that it wasn't a nail, it was a worm. He had poured some chemicals over the worm and it got as hard as a nail. The father said, "Give me the chemicals and I'll give you a Volkswagen." The next day Johnny went into the garage and saw a Mercedes-Benz. He asked his father where the Volkswagen was, and the father said that the Volkswagen was in front of the Mercedes and that the Mercedes was from his mother!

* * *

How can a real man tell if his girlfriend's having an orgasm?

Real men don't care!

* * *

An explorer/animal trapper was on an expedition in deepest, darkest Africa capturing gorillas. What he would do was climb a gorilla-inhabited tree and shake it hard, and ultimately a gorilla would fall out. Immediately his trained Doberman pinscher would bite the gorilla in his private parts, the gorilla would throw up his hands and the trapper would run in and handcuff the gorilla. Eventually they caught and handcuffed several gorillas this way. A man asked the explorer, "Well, why does that trapper of yours carry a gun?" The explorer replied, "In case I fall out of the tree, he's there to shoot the dog!"

Did you hear about the guy who got his vasectomy done at Sears?

Every time he gets a hard-on, the garage door goes up.

* * *

Why is it so great to be a test-tube baby?

Because you get a womb with a view!

* * *

What do elephants use for condoms?

Goodyear blimps!

* * *

What do you call a midget psychic who just committed a crime?

A small medium at large.

* * *

What's the definition of macho?

Jogging home from your own vasectomy.

* * *

Why did God create man?

Because you can't teach an electric vibrator to mow the lawn!

* * *

How can you tell when an elephant has its period?

You wake up, your mattress is gone and there's a dime under your pillow!

* * *

What do you get when you mix holy water with castor oil?

A religious movement!

Why is it a drag to screw a cow?
　You have to climb down from the stump and walk around front every time you want to kiss her.

* * *

Did you hear about the new designer condoms?
　They're called "Sergio Prevente"!

* * *

Why is there so little fraternizing on naval ships?
　Because sailors seldom see each other face to face!

* * *

Where does virgin wool come from?
　From sheep the herder couldn't catch.

* * *

Why don't pygmies wear tampons?
　They keep stepping on the string.

* * *

What's the difference between mono and herpes?
　You get mono from snatching a kiss!

* * *

If our ancestors came over on a boat, how did herpes come over?
　On the captain's dinghy!

* * *

Why is pubic hair curly?
　If it was straight, it would poke your eyes out!

* * *

What's the definition of a perfect woman?
　One that, after you're done screwing, turns into a six-pack and three of your best friends.

Why do women have two holes?

So that when they get drunk you can carry them home like a six-pack.

* * *

What's the difference between a gynecologist and a genealogist?

A genealogist looks up your family tree, and a gynecologist looks up your family bush.

* * *

Why are cowgirls bowlegged?

Because cowboys like to eat with their hats on.

* * *

Daddy, what's a clitoris?

You should have asked me last night. I had it on the tip of my tonque!

* * *

This old man, Abe, and his elderly wife, Becky, are in bed together. And Becky says, "Abe, Abe, I'm dying, I'm dying." Abe says, "Oh, I'm sorry to hear that. Is there anything that I can do to help you?" And she says, "Abe, there's only one thing. In all the years we've been together and having sex, we never once had anal intercourse." Abe says, "If this is what you want, I'll do it!"

So they have sex together, and Abe falls asleep, and the next morning he wakes up, and he hears that Becky is out in the kitchen cooking breakfast. He looks at her, and she's got a smile on her face. And she says, "Abe, Abe, come and have some breakfast." And Abe starts to cry. And Becky says, "Abe,

Abe, I feel wonderful!" And Abe cries and cries. So she says, "Abe, what's wrong?" He says, "I know you feel wonderful. But if I had known it would help, I could have saved Mother and Father!"

* * *

Did you hear what the next generation of Swedes are going to be like?

They'll have blonde eyes and blue hair!

* * *

What do Tylenol, NASA and a walrus have in common?

They're all looking for a tighter seal!

* * *

A girl is getting married, and her father is very upset. She has a long-standing heart problem, and he wants to be sure she's warned her husband-to-be that it exists. So the day of the wedding, he takes the guy aside and says, "Listen. I don't know if she's told you this, but I think you ought to know. My daughter has acute angina." The guy grins at him and says, "Boy, that's good, because she sure don't have no tits!"

* * *

To restore a sense of reality to amusement parks, I think Walt Disney should have a HARD-LUCK LAND. There the visitor could fall in love and get his first "Dear John" letter, receive draft and induction notices, fall behind on new car payments, learn that his brother-in-law and five children are coming to spend their vacation with him, and learn that his father is secretly screwing his aunt!

What did the leper say to the prostitute?
I left you the tip!

* * *

An eighty-seven-year-old man goes to the doctor and says, "Doctor, Doctor, I can't pee!" The doctor says, "How old are you?" He says, "Eighty-seven years old." The doctor says, "You've peed enough!"

* * *

What's the difference between a pussy and a cunt?
A pussy's soft and sweet. A cunt is the person who owns it!

* * *

This guy goes to a doctor. The doctor says, "Have you ever had this before?" "Yes," says the guy. "Well," says the doctor, "you've got it again!"

* * *

A woman walks into a bar and says to the bartender, "Give me a beer, please."
She can't believe it when the guy says to her, "Anheuser Busch?"
"And how's your cock?" she demands.

* * *

This guy dies with a hard-on, so the undertaker calls his wife and says he can't close the casket; what should he do?
The woman says, "Cut his dick off and shove it up his ass. He was very much into anal sex with me!"
So the undertaker prepares the corpse as instructed and arranges for the viewing. The people at the fun-

eral approach the corpse and notice a slight grin on its face. As a matter of fact, some of them even comment on this sadistic smile. The wife finally approaches the corpse of her husband, notices his grin, looks at him and says,

"Hurts, doesn't it!"

* * *

This guy is forty-five years old. He goes to his doctor and says, "Doc, it's time I was circumcised."

They arrange it, and the guy goes in and has his surgery done. When he wakes up afterward, the doctor is standing there and he's very contrite. "I have good news and bad news," says the doctor. "The bad news is, the knife slipped."

"Oh, no!" says the guy. "Well, tell me the good news."

"The good news is, it wasn't malignant!"

* * *

There's a new dildo salesman in the store, and the boss has him on trial to see if he is good at sales. The guy gets his first customer: a white girl who asks for a dildo. The salesman says, "We have white dildos for $50 and black dildos for $60." The girl buys a black dildo. The next customer comes in: a black girl. The salesman says, "We have black dildos for $50 and white dildos for $60." She buys the white dildo. The next customer is Polish, and he asks for a dildo. "We have black dildos for $50, white dildos for $60, and plaid dildos for $75." The Polack takes the plaid dildo. The boss comes back and asks how everything is going. "Great," says the salesman. "I sold a black dildo for $60, a white dildo for $60, and I sold my Thermos bottle for $75!"

Two women were talking, and one asked the other, "Do you smoke when you have sex?"

"I don't know," the other woman said. "I've never looked!"

* * *

My heart belongs to another, but the rest of me is open for an offer!

* * *

Isn't that sweet? He's trying to make me feel at home — and he is.

I have a miserable home!

* * *

This woman goes into a bar and says to the bartender, "Give me three double shots of gin!" The bartender gives the woman the shots; she drinks them immediately and promptly passes out on the floor. The bartender goes around the bar, checks her out and notices that her dress is hiked up a little so he admires her beautiful legs. He decides to give it to her right there, and does. A customer in the bar observes this, comes over and decides to slip it to her too. The bartender and the customer then decide to call a cab. The cab driver arrives, takes her into his vehicle, notices her beauty and decides to give it to her too.

The woman returns to the bar the next day, same time, and orders from the same bartender three double shots of Scotch. The bartender says, "I thought you liked gin?"

"I tried it," says the woman, "but it makes me sore!"

One prostitute says to the other, "I made $400 last night."

"Gross?" the other asks.

"No, Schwartz!"

* * *

Two men are sitting down in a bar together, and one guy says to the other, "You're really ugly!" The second guy says, "You're really drunk!" The drunk one says, "You know, the more I look at you, the uglier you get." The second guy says, "I'm going to tell you one more time. You are really drunk, and I'm getting tired of listening to you." The drunk guy says, "Yeah, right, but tomorrow morning, see, *I'm* gonna be sober!"

* * *

A mouse used to live in a winery, and he would climb up on the rim of a vat and run around and around the edge. One day he finally slipped and fell into the vat full of wine. He couldn't get out again, so he swam around in the wine and shouted, "Help! Help!" A cat heard the mouse's cries for help, climbed up onto the rim and sat looking down at him. The mouse cried, "Please, Mr. Cat, help me! I'm drowning!" The cat said, "Well, if I save you, what do I get?" The mouse said, "Anything! Help me!" The cat said, "Well, if I save you, can I eat you?" The mouse said, "Yes! Yes! Anything you want!" So the cat reached down with his paw and hooked the mouse back up to safety. The mouse immediately shook himself dry and then darted back into his hole. The cat said, "Mr. Mouse, you're not keeping your word! You said I could eat you!" The mouse said, "Well, Mr. Cat, what do you expect? I was drunk at the time!"

* * *

This couple had a nip-and-tuck marriage. The man was always taking a nip, and his wife was always tucking him in.

* * *

Then there was this other couple who had a beef-stew marriage. She was always beefing, and he was always stewed!

* * *

A guy is sitting in a bar with his twelve-inch pianist sitting on his shoulder. He orders a drink from the bartender, and the bartender says, "Where'd you get this wise-ass little twelve-inch pianist?" "Well," the man says, "I was at the beach the other day, and I found an Aladdin's lamp, rubbed it and a genie came out. And the genie gave me three wishes. My first wish was to have a million dollars. My second wish was to have a beautiful home." The bartender says, "And your third wish was to have a twelve-inch pianist?"

"Well," the man says, "not exactly!"

* * *

This man had a weight problem, and he tried many conceivable methods of weight loss and spent several hundred dollars trying to lose weight. He was about to give up when one day he saw an advertisement that said, GUARANTEED WEIGHT LOSS OF 20-50 POUNDS IN JUST 2 SESSIONS OR YOUR MONEY BACK!

The man said, "Well, I've tried so many of these things and nothing's worked. But what have I got to lose?" So he went to the place and talked with the manager, and the manager said, "Yes! We absolutely guarantee that you can lose forty pounds in just two sessions or your money back!" So the guy said, "Okay, I'll try it. What do I gotta do?" The manager said, "All you gotta do is go upstairs and take the first door on your left. Go inside, take off all your clothes and relax." So the fat guy went upstairs and through the door and found a completely empty room, with only a bed standing right in the middle of it. The man got undressed and sat down on the bed. All of a sudden a beautiful woman appeared — completely naked except for a sign around her neck that read: IF YOU CAN CATCH ME, YOU CAN FUCK ME. So the fat man said, "Why not?" And he proceeded to chase the woman around and around the room. He ran and ran and ran, chasing this woman until suddenly, just as mysteriously as she appeared, the woman disappeared. The man wiped the sweat from his brow and noticed half an hour had passed. He got dressed, went downstairs, weighed himself and saw that he had lost twenty pounds! "All right!" said the fat guy.

He paid the manager his $50 fee, arranged to have his second session the very next day and went home feeling very happy. Now that he'd lost all that weight, he was positive that he could catch the girl. So the next day the guy came back to the establishment. The manager said, "Go back to the same room and take off your clothes again, just like you did before." "That's all?" asked the guy. "That's all," said the manager. So the fat guy went upstairs, went into

the room, took off all his clothes and sat down.
All of a sudden, out of nowhere, appeared a six-
foot gorilla with a sign around his neck saying, IF
I CATCH YOU, I GET TO FUCK YOU. So the guy freaked
out and ran all over the room to escape the gorilla.
And he ran and ran and ran, and just when he was
almost exhausted — the gorilla disappeared. So the
guy wiped the sweat from his brow, got dressed and
went downstairs. He weighed himself and found out
that he had lost another twenty pounds!" "Oh, wow!"
said the no-longer-fat guy, and he paid the final $50,
thanked the manager and went home, very happy
with himself.

* * *

There is a man on a deserted island who was shipwrecked twenty years ago. He hasn't seen anyone, man
or woman, for twenty years. Suddenly, out of the
water appears a voluptuous blonde. She's wearing
a wet suit, and she walks up to the guy and he's
rubbing his eyes in disbelief. She says, "How would
you like a cigarette?" Well, the guy was a chain smok-
er before he was shipwrecked, so he says, "I'd *love*
a cigarette. I haven't tasted tobacco in twenty years!
Oh, how I'd love a cigarette." So she unzips the
zipper on her wet suit a little bit, takes out a pack
of cigarettes, puts a cigarette in his mouth and lights
it up for him. He's enjoying the smoke and she says,
"How would you like a martini?" He says, "Oh, I'd
love a martini! That was my favorite drink. I haven't
tasted alcohol in twenty years!" So she unzips her
wet suit a little bit more, exposing more of her cleav-
age, and she reaches in and pulls out a bottle of
gin, some ice, and a mixing glass. She shakes it up,

strains out the martini into a glass and gives it to him. So he's sipping it up, enjoying his drink and his cigarette, and the girl unzips her wet suit a little more. She looks at him with a gleam in her eye, and she says, "How would you like to play around?" And the guy says, "Don't tell me you've got a set of golf clubs in there too!"

* * *

A young couple is in dire financial straits, and they've tried every way to earn money. So finally the husband sits down with his loving wife — she's a rather plain woman — and he says, "Honey, the only way I think we can make any more money is if you go out in the street and sell your body." Well, at first the wife is a little hesitant about it, but finally she agrees. So she goes out the first day, and she comes home beaming and he says, "Well, honey, how much did you make today?" And she says, "Fifty dollars and twenty-five cents." And the guy says, "Fifty dollars and twenty-five cents? Who gave you the quarter?" She says, "Everybody!"

* * *

A girl had the largest pussy in the world. She meets this guy, a Texan, in a bar and she says, "Tex, I got the biggest hole in the world! Why don't you get your biggest cowboy boots and come up to my room with me?" So the Texan goes to her room, and he's got his big cowboy hat on, and he's got his two big boots in his hands, and he says, "These are Size Thirteen EEE. I bet you can't get the big toe of one of these fuckers up there!" So she says, "Try me, Tex." And she lies down on the bed, spreads her legs high up in the air, and the Texan brings up his big boot. He slides the whole thing right in and he says, "Oh, my God, we got a big one here!" He takes the other boot and pushes it in a little bit, and the whole thing slides right in! The woman says, "Tex, I didn't even *feel* that!" So Tex says, "Well, try this." So he bends over and sticks his whole head in there, and before he knows it, he's got one shoulder in, and he falls inside her pussy! So he's inside her pussy, groping around, and he brings out his flashlight and looks around, and he sees there's another guy in there with him! Tex says, "Hey! What are *you* doing in here!" And the guy says, "I got in here the same way you did!" So Tex says, "Well, it's a good thing I got this flashlight, so we can find our way out of here." The other guy replies, "Let's look around a little first. If we find my car keys, we can *drive* out of here!"

* * *

Three guys who work in an office are boasting about their sexual exploits, and they're talking about penis size and so on, and one of them says, "Oh, I've got the longest penis around." The second says, "No you don't, mine's longer than yours." And the third guy says, "No, *mine* is the longest!" So one says, "Look. This building is twenty stories high. Why don't we go up to the roof of the building, drop our penises over the side and that way we'll be able to measure who has the longest." So they do. The first guy unzips his fly and throws his penis over the side of the building, and it goes down two whole stories, to the eighteenth floor. The second guy says, "Oh, I got you beat." He unzips his fly, throws his penis over the side of the building and it falls all the way down to the fifteenth floor. So they look around for the third guy, and they finally spot him over in the corner. He'd unzipped his fly and let his penis out, and he was dancing up and down. The other two guys said, "Hey, what are you doing?" "Dodging traffic," the guy replied.

* * *

This man goes to a doctor and says, "Doctor, I'm having a little problem with my penis, and I'd like you to take a look at it." So the doctor says okay, and checks it out. To the doctor's amazement, he sees that on the man's penis he has tattooed TINY. The doctor is so astounded that he has to excuse himself, and he goes out and tells his nurse. The nurse is a voluptuous blonde woman, and the doctor says to her, "Nurse, you won't believe what this man has tattooed on his penis. You've got to see it for yourself — he has TINY tattooed on his penis." So the nurse goes into the room with the patient and comes out a few minutes later with a big smile on her face. She says, "You ought to look more closely, Doctor. It didn't say TINY, it said TICONDEROGA, NY!"

Part Two
FOOD JOKES!

THE WORST DIET YOU EVER READ!

What did the egg say to the boiling water?
    How do you expect me to get hard when I just got laid!

* * *

    She used to diet on any kind of food she could lay her hands on!

* * *

What's the scoop?
    Don't be a dip. What do you think this is, an ice cream parlor?

* * *

Did you hear about the two peanuts that walked across Central Park?
    One was a salted.

He bites his nails so much his stomach needs a manicure!

* * *

This doctor orders a daiquiri with a walnut in it every day at a bar. One day there are no walnuts, so the bartender puts a hickory nut in it. The doctor looks at his drink and says, "What's this?" The bartender says, "Oh, that's a hickory daiquiri, Doc."

* * *

Do you like turkey?
Gobble this.

* * *

My milkman really got a shock the other day. For ten years he always left a quart of milk at the widow's house next door. Every day, the same thing. Quart of milk. No more, no less. Then last week he finds a note next to the back door which says he should leave ten gallons. Well, thinking something must be wrong, the milkman knocks on the door to check. Sure enough, the old lady says she wants ten gallons of milk. It seems she heard that taking a bath in milk would improve her health, and she wanted the ten gallons for a milk bath. "Well, okay," agreed the milkman. "You want it pasteurized?"

"No," the old lady replied. "Just past my tits."

* * *

There are two things in the world that smell like fish.
Fish is one of them.

What can you use used tampons for?
    Tea bags for vampires!

* * *

If a savage swallowed a pine cone, what would it be called?
    Cone in the Barbarian.

* * *

Did you ever hear of garlic pizza?
    No, but I'm getting wind of it!

* * *

This man has a double chin — it was too much work for one!

* * *

Is the fat kid looking?
    Ram a spoon in his mouth or he'll eat his chin!

* * *

There's a new reducing pill with sleeping tablet — for people who like light naps!

* * *

REDUCING SALON
A place that takes your wife's breadth away!

* * *

My stomach is back to that "dunlap" stage again — dun lapped over my belt!

* * *

A lady came out of a supermarket and dropped her package containing one bottle of ketchup and two eggs. A drunk came over and said, "Don't worry, lady. He wouldn't have lived anyway. His eyes are too far apart!"

WHAT DO YOU CALL ...

What do soybeans and dildos have in common?
Both are meat substitutes!

* * *

What do you call a cow with an abortion?
Decalfinated!

* * *

Why don't chickens wear underwear?
Because their peckers are on their faces!

* * *

What's invisible and smells like carrots?
Bunny farts!

* * *

What do you call a herd of masturbating cattle?
Beef Strokinoff!

* * *

What do you get when you cross an onion and a jackass?
A piece of ass that will bring tears to your eyes.

* * *

What goes in hard and pink and comes out soft and mushy?
Bubble gum!

What do you call a legless steer?
Ground beef!

* * *

What can a lifesaver do that a man can't do?
Come in five flavors.

* * *

If the Lord had not wanted man to eat pussy, he wouldn't have made it look so much like a taco!

* * *

A husband is on his way to the office when he realizes he forgot his briefcase. He goes home, goes up to his bedroom, and sees his wife naked with her back to him, taking some money out of his briefcase. He sneaks up behind her, pats her on the ass and says, "How much today, honey?"
The wife doesn't even turn around and says, "Four quarts of milk and a dozen eggs."

* * *

What's the difference between erotic and kinky?
When it's erotic you use a feather, and when it's kinky you use the whole chicken!

* * *

Did you hear about the new gourmet restaurant on Mars?
Fabulous food, no atmosphere!

* * *

Why do farts smell?
So deaf people can enjoy them too!

Why does an egg have a terrible life?
— The only one that sits on its face is its mother!
— You only get laid once!
— It takes at least three minutes to get hard!
— You come in a box with eleven others!

* * *

What's the difference between a proctologist and a mixologist?
A proctologist only deals with one asshole at a time!

* * *

What's green and red and goes 1,000 mph?
A frog in a blender!

* * *

What's the best thing to give an eighty-year-old woman?
Little Mikey — he'll eat anything.

* * *

What do they call kids born in whorehouses?
Brothel sprouts.

* * *

What's green and makes holes?
A drill pickle.

* * *

What's the difference between an oral and a rectal thermometer?
The taste.

* * *

What's yellow and green and eats nuts?
Gonorrhea.

What's green and smells like pork?
Kermit's finger.

* * *

My doctor told me to stop all drinks. I do! I never let a drink get past me!

* * *

My doctor told me not to drink anymore. So I don't. But I don't drink any less!

* * *

Two Scotsmen are killing me!
Haig and Haig.

* * *

This guy goes out and buys his mother a very expensive birthday present: a beautiful parrot that speaks five languages and cost $1,000. He pays for the bird and has it delivered to her apartment. Later on he drops by and says, "Did you get my present?" Yes!" says his mother, "and, son, I must say, it was delicious!" "Delicious!" he says. "Mother! That was a very expensive bird — it spoke five languages!" "So?" says the old lady. "It spoke five languages? Then why didn't it say something!"

* * *

This man has a terrible weight problem, so he goes to a doctor and says, "Doc, I want to lose weight. What can I do?" And the doctor says, "Well, you can eat anything you want as long as you eat it anally." The guy says, "Okay." So he comes back a couple of weeks later, and he's really thin, and he's moving both legs up and down almost as if he's walking in place. The man says, "Thanks, Doc. I've lost a lot of weight." And the doctor says, "Well, you look great. But what are you doing?" "Chewing gum."

* * *

An American businessman is in Spain for the first time, and he takes in a lot of the culture of Spain and goes to a bullfight. After the bullfight, he's a little bit hungry, so he makes his way down to a local cantina and orders what Americans usually order. The waiter, however, insists that he try the day's special. So he asks the waiter, "What is the day's special?" And the waiter replies, "Bull's balls." And the American says, "Bull's balls! That doesn't sound too appealing." The waiter says, "Oh no, *señor*! It is the sweetest meat, the most succulent. You'll love it." So the guy thinks, "Well, Jeez, I'm in Spain; I might as well adapt to the customs." And he orders it. Sure enough, it is the sweetest, most succulent, tastiest meat he's ever eaten in his life. He loves it and he gives the waiter a very big-time tip. The very next day he runs into a friend of his named Charlie. He says, "Charlie, you've gotta come with me to this little cantina. It is fantastic. They have a great special there, and I want you to try it." So they go in and the guy says, "Waiter, two specials." And the waiter says, "Oh yes, *señor*." And the waiter brings the specials over, takes the lids off the dishes and serves them. Well, it is the most rancid, the rudest meat he's ever eaten in his life. He calls the waiter over and he says, "*Señor*, yesterday when I came in, you told me to order the special, and it was the sweetest, most succulent meat I've ever eaten in my entire life. And today

I ordered the bull's balls for myself and my friend here, and it's the worst-tasting meat I've ever had. What's happened?" The waiter says, "Oh, *señor*, it's very simple. *Yesterday* was the bull's balls special. But today, it is not the bull's balls. After all, *señor*, the bullfighter, he not always win."

Part Three

HOLLYWEIRD

Jokes about Hollywood, Los Angeles and the Entertainment Industry

She wears a sweater marked,
MADE IN HOLLYWOOD BY ALMOST EVERYBODY!

* * *

It was a great film festival at Cannes last year — six starlets pushed a naked press agent into a pool!

* * *

You can tell the economy's booming again.
Yes-men in Hollywood are getting so independent they're only nodding!

* * *

Mae West had an eighty-year-old boyfriend who had a twenty-year-old girlfriend. Mae said that was great but that she had a twenty-year-old boyfriend, and twenty goes into eighty a hell of a lot more than eighty into twenty.

Hollywood is only the glitter of false tinsel.
If you peel away the false tinsel, there's real tinsel underneath!

* * *

You can stuff all the sincerity in Hollywood in a flea's navel . . . and still have room for eight caraway seeds and an agent's heart!

* * *

HOLLYWOOD — a place where, if an actor's wife looks like a new woman, she probably is!

* * *

What's the difference between a porcupine and a Porsche?
On the porcupine the pricks are on the outside.

* * *

An associate producer is the only guy in Hollywood who will associate with a producer!

* * *

Hollywood is a place where people from Iowa mistake each other for movie stars!

* * *

Hollywood is no place for a professional comedian. The amateur competition is too great!

* * *

I knew a luscious young dish who went to Hollywood because she wanted to make love under the stars!

A recent independent survey indicated that it's still possible for a young woman with little or no experience to *make* her way into show business!

* * *

Hollywood is the city where they put beautiful frames in pictures!

* * *

Gypsy Rose Lee, the strip-tease artist, arrived in Hollywood with twelve empty trunks!

* * *

Did you hear about the new nature movie?
The epic story of a neurotic salmon who only wants to float downstream!

* * *

If you're ever in Hollywood, stop in and use my pool — I'd *love* to give you drowning lessons!

* * *

This producer had a secretary who was getting a little behind at work, and a wife who was getting a big one at home!

* * *

DIRECTOR: "I want to see zip in this performance! I want pizzazz! I want vigor!"

ASSISTANT: "Okay, sir. Zip, Pizzazz and Vigor — *on stage!*"

* * *

A bookseller admits to having been momentarily taken aback when an aspiring young actress asked for a volume she titled, "How to Make Friends and Influential People"!

* * *

What's red and has seven dents?
  Snow White's cherry!

* * *

What's a constipated accountant do?
  He works it out with his pencil!

* * *

Did you hear about the new movie that Sylvester Stallone and Matt Dillon are starring in?
  It's the first English-language film to be completely subtitled!

* * *

What do the Yankees and Michael Jackson have in common?
  They both wear one glove for no apparent reason!

* * *

How many actors does it take to change a light bulb?
  A thousand! One to change the light bulb, and 999 to say, "I could have done that."

* * *

How can you tell when an entertainment lawyer is lying?
  His lips are moving!

* * *

What do you need when you have three entertainment lawyers up to their necks in cement?
  More cement!

What is this? 9, 8, 7, 6, 5, 4, 3, 2, 1, 0.

Bo Derek's career since *10*!

* * *

What's the difference between the Super Bowl and the Space Shuttle of 1986?

They were both great for the first seventy-one seconds!

* * *

HOLLYWOOD: Where else can you go out on a blind date and end up with your wife?!

* * *

#1: How did you get in?

#2: With a friend's ticket.

#1: Where's your friend?

#2: Home looking for his ticket!

* * *

A film director went to heaven, and an angel was showing him around the film-production facilities there, which were state of the art. He was extremely impressed with all the equipment. The director then said, "I wonder what hell's facilities look like? Can you show me?" So the angel took the director to hell, and the director was amazed with the facilities, as they were comparable with heaven's. The director asked the angel what the difference between heaven's and hell's facilities were. The angel answered, "Well, in heaven films get made!"

* * *

A man is walking around in Hollywood, and he comes to this building and spots a man who looks like a doctor. The man says to the doctor, "What goes on in here?" The doctor says, "This is a research institute, and we use lawyers instead of guinea pigs for testing." The man says, "Why do you use lawyers?" The doctor says, "Well, two reasons: number one, there are so many of them. And number two, you don't get attached to them!"

* * *

Show me a person who lives in Hollywood who says that "Talk is cheap" and I'll show you a person who's never been to a Beverly Hills psychiatrist!

* * *

I was making this deal with an agent one day, optioning a screenplay, and he said to me, "Every time I say okay, you say okay. Okay?" "Okay." "Okay!" "Okay!" "Okay!!" "Okay!!"

* * *

This Hollywood millionaire made a killing on entertainment stocks! He murdered his broker!

* * *

What did Loretta Swit and Richard Pryor have in common?
    They both had major burns on their face!

* * *

What do seven-foot basketball players do in off-season?
    Go to the movies and sit in front of you!

* * *

Why can't you go to the bathroom at a Beatles concert?
    There's no John!

Why are the Rams changing their names to the Tampons?

They're only good for one period, and they have no second string.

* * *

How can you tell a DeLorean driving down the street?

The white line disappears.

* * *

What kind of tires do DeLoreans have?

Snow tires.

* * *

What's blue and sings alone?

Dan Aykroyd!

* * *

What's the difference between a moose and Guy Lombardo's orchestra?

With a moose the horns are in the front and the asshole's in the rear.

* * *

What happened to the pope when he went to Mount Olive?

Popeye almost killed him.

* * *

These three producers go to heaven, and the first one is interviewed by Saint Peter. Saint Peter says, "Have you ever cheated on your wife?" And the man says, "Saint Peter, I've never, ever cheated on my wife and I've been totally faithful." And Saint Peter says, "Are you sure you're telling me the truth?" And the man says, "Absolutely." So Saint Peter says, "See this set of gold keys? Why don't you go over there and drive that Cadillac around? It's yours for being so honest and faithful to your wife." "Thank you!" says the man. The next producer comes up and Saint Peter interviews him and says, "Have you ever cheated on your wife?" And the man says, "Yes, sir, I must admit I cheated on my wife once, but after I got it out of my system I was totally faithful." And Saint Peter says, "Okay, I believe you. You see this set of keys here? Why don't you go over there and drive that Honda around. It's the silver one — the same color as the keys." And the guy says, "Oh, only a Honda? Oh, well, thank you." And he drives off. The third producer comes up, and Saint Peter says, "Have you ever cheated on your wife?" And the man says, "Saint, I must confess, I have cheated on my wife dozens of times. I am a proverbial skirt chaser, and I am not a monogamous man at all." Saint Peter says, "Well, it's terrible that you were such a promiscuous man. However, you've been honest in confessing this to me. You see this key? You see that pair of roller skates over there? They are yours." And the man says, "I only get a pair of roller skates?!" "Here they are," insists Saint Peter. So the man goes roller-skating around heaven, and all of a sudden the gold Cadillac approaches him. Producer number three looks at producer number one and notices he has a terrible frown on his face. So he roller-skates up to him and says, "What's wrong with you?" And the man says, "I just saw my wife go by on a pair of roller skates."

Did you hear about the rich Texas producer who bought his dog a little boy!

* * *

The producer likes to see a broad smile — when she's smiling at him!

* * *

These two producers, Robert and Alfred, have been in business a long time. Robert is dying of food poisoning, and he says to Alfred, "Alfred, we've been in business a long time, and before I die I have to clear my conscience. Do you remember when that money was missing from the safe and we never found who stole it? Alfred, it was me that took the money. And do you remember all the nights that your wife came home late, or didn't come home at all, with some weak excuse afterward? Alfred, your wife and I were shacking up together for years." Alfred says to Robert, "Robert, don't you think I know this? Who do you think gave you the poison?"

* * *

Why did Arnold Schwarzenegger marry Maria Shriver?
   So they could breed bullet-proof entities!

* * *

How many directors does it take to screw in a light bulb?
   None. Directors screw in hot tubs.

* * *

How many Californians does it take to screw in a light bulb?

Three. One to stand on the ladder and two to experience it.

* * *

What does an actress put behind her legs to impress a producer?
Her ankles!

* * *

Did you hear that Prince Rainier finally got some good news?
The car was covered by insurance.

* * *

Who taught Grace Kelly how to drive?
Ted Kennedy.

* * *

What do toilet paper and the starship Enterprise have in common?
They both circle Uranus looking for Klingons.

* * *

One day the Lone Ranger was captured by the Indians, and they said, "You're a very famous man, so before we kill you we're going to give you one last wish." "Okay," said the Ranger, "can I please speak to my horse?" And the Indians said all right. So the Lone Ranger called, "Hi-ho, Silver!" Silver galloped up and the Ranger whispered in his ear, and Silver promptly took off and came back with a beautiful, voluptuous woman, to whom the Lone Ranger immediately made mad, passionate love, right in front of the Indians.

The Indians were extremely impressed with this event and said, "Now that you've done this, we respect you so much that we're going to give you one more last wish." So the Lone Ranger said again, "May I speak to my horse?" And again the Indians said yes. So the Lone Ranger called, "Hi-ho, Silver!" Silver appeared, and the Lone Ranger leaned in real close and whispered into his ear, "I said, 'posse,' idiot, 'posse'!"

* * *

This Indian actor goes to a department store to buy some toilet paper, and asks, "Me want four rolls that toilet paper." The store manager says, "Okay, Injun, that will be $6." The Indian says, "Too much money. Have other kind of paper?" The manager says, "Yes. We have toilet paper with no name outside the package, four rolls for $2." The Indian says, "Okay, take it. Take paper. But why that one less?" And the store manager says, "Because it doesn't have a name on the outside of the package." And the Indian says, "Okay, take paper."

A couple of days later the Indian comes back to the store and says to the manager, "I know what to call paper I buy from you." The manager says, "What do you call it?" The Indian says, "John Wayne toilet paper." The manager says, "Why do you call it John Wayne toilet paper?" And the Indian says, "Because it rough, tough and take no shit off Indian!

* * *

This actress is the type who likes to be taken with a grain of assault!

SOME LEADING PAPERS' COVERAGE OF CUSTER'S MASSACRE

Variety: "Custer Closes Out of Town"
Pravda: "Big Red Victory"
Sports Illustrated: "Indians Win Series"
Women's Wear Daily: "Feathers Make Comeback"
Reader's Digest: "Sitting Bull Reveals New Cure for
                   Dandruff"
The Washington Post: "Custer Loses Rural Vote"

Part Four
ETHNIC JOKES

Ethnic Hollywood

If Tarzan and Jane were Italian, what would Cheetah be?

The other woman.

* * *

If Tarzan and Jane were Polish, what would Cheetah be?

Their gifted child.

* * *

If Tarzan and Jane were Jewish, what would Cheetah be?

Her fur.

* * *

What do you get when you cross a black man with Bo Derek?

A ten of spades.

Did you hear about the new movie that Mel Brooks is producing starring Michael Jackson and Richard Pryor?

It's called *Blazing Sambos*!

* * *

Did you hear that the Ku Klux Klan bought the movie rights to *Roots*?

They're going to play it backward so it will have a happy ending!

* * *

Gay actors are having a lot of difficulty getting auto insurance out west.

They've been rear-ended too many times.

* * *

What do you call two gay men named Bob?

Oral Roberts!

* * *

What's the difference between a producer and a homo?

A producer doesn't have any friends at all, and a homo has friends up the ass.

* * *

What do you call a couple of gay Hollywood lawyers?

Legal Aids.

* * *

An Italian actor was going to star in *Beverly Hills Cop* before Eddie Murphy got the part.

It was going to be called *Beverly Hills Wop*.

Did you hear about the two major Italian producers who were partners?

Dino went to the office and called Carlo and said, "We've been robbed!"

Carlo said, "Dino, put the money back!"

* * *

There's a new movie out about a JAP. She lost all her money and had to fire her maid. It's called *Debby Does Dishes*.

* * *

An Italian actor and a Polish actor are parachuting. The Pole jumps and his parachute opens. The Italian jumps and his parachute doesn't open and he passes the Pole when falling. The Pole thinks he wants to race and throws away his parachute.

* * *

Did you hear about the Polish actress who flew to Hollywood from New York?

She went there to sleep with a writer!

* * *

Where can a woman buy panties made out of fertilizer bags, and bras made out of beer cans?

Frederick's of Poland!

* * *

What do you call two Vietnamese in a Trans-Am?

The Gooks of Hazard.

* * *

Buckwheat grew up and joined the Muslim faith, and when he joined it he changed his name. What is he called now?

Kareem of Wheat!

What do you get when you cross a gorilla with an Italian actor?

A dirty look from the gorilla!

Black Jokes

What do the post office and Kinney Shoes have in common?
  Both have 30,000 black loafers!

* * *

Why do black guys wear high-heeled shoes?
  To keep from scraping their knuckles when they walk.

* * *

What was the first black test-tube baby called?
  Janitor in a drum!

* * *

What's black and white and red all over?
  An interracial couple in an automobile accident.

What's the definition of black foreplay?
Don't scream or I'll kill you.

* * *

What do you call a black man in a tree?
Branch manager.

* * *

This man goes to a doctor and says, "Doctor, I need a new dick."
The doctor says, "No problem, we have three kinds. We have a three and a half inch, five and a half inch, and a nine incher. Which one would you like?"
The man says, "May I see the nine incher?"
The doctor says, "No problem."
The man says, "But, Doc, could I have it in white?"

* * *

Who are the two most famous black women in history?
Aunt Jemima and Mutha Fucka.

* * *

What's the difference between a bowling ball and a black woman?
If you really had to, you could eat a bowling ball!

* * *

What's the most confusing day in Harlem?
Father's Day!

* * *

BLACK: "We're not struggling to be free — we want to get paid!"

How does God make Puerto Ricans?
By sandblasting blacks.

* * *

After the Reverend Jesse Jackson brought back
Robert Goodman, the reporters asked the reverend
how he liked Beirut.
"Okay," said Jackson, "but I like Hank Aaron
better."

* * *

What's black and white, black and white, black and
white and red?
A black and a pelican fighting over a carp.

* * *

Nerve is starting a KKK chapter in Ghana.

* * *

Why are black people sexually obsessed?
If you had pubic hair on your head, you'd be
sexually obsessed too.

* * *

What do you get when you cross a gay Eskimo and
a black?
A snowblower that doesn't work!

* * *

Why don't black women make good nuns?
They can't say superior after mother!

* * *

Do you know why blacks don't let their babies play
in sandboxes?
Because the cats keep trying to cover them up!

Why did God invent the climax?
So blacks would know when to stop fucking!

* * *

How do you make a black person nervous?
Take him to an auction!

* * *

Why do blacks keep chickens?
To teach their kids how to walk!

* * *

If you throw a black person and a log off a cliff, which one lands first?
Who cares!

* * *

What do you get when you cross a black guy and a Sioux Indian?
A Sioux named Boy.

* * *

What do you get when you cross a black guy with a Japanese guy?
A guy who, every December 7, has this uncontrollable urge to attack Pearl Bailey.

* * *

Three black girls are sitting around talking about their boyfriends, and one says, "I calls my boyfriend 86 because he's eight inches long and six inches around." The next girl says, "I calls my boyfriend 27 because he's two times a day, seven day a week." The last girl says, "I calls my boyfriend Drambuie."

And the others ask, "Why you call him Drambuie? That sounds like a liquor." And the last girl says, "That's him!"

* * *

This white traveling salesman is traveling in Mississippi, down an old country road, and he's going very fast because there's no traffic around. So he's rounding a corner at about 60 mph when suddenly there are two blacks by the side of the road. He can't swerve out of the way to avoid them, so he runs into them. One of the blacks comes through the window and lands in the back seat; the other flies seventy feet into a field. Just as the accident occurs, a state trooper appears on the scene. The guy is really distraught, and he says, "I'm sorry, Officer, I'm so sorry. I saw them at the last minute, and there was nothing I could do." The cop says, "Now, don't worry about it a bit, son. We'll get this one in the back seat for breaking and entering, and the other one for leaving the scene of the accident!"

* * *

Is it better to be born black or gay?
Black, because you don't have to tell your parents.

Gay Jokes

How many gays does it take to change a light bulb?
Ten! One to put in the bulb, and nine to say *fabulous*.

* * *

What is it called when you have your tonsils out?
A tonsillectomy.
What is it called when a woman is fixed?
A hysterectomy.
What is it called when a man is fixed?
A vasectomy.
What is it called when a woman gets changed to a man?
Addadicktome.

* * *

What is a bisexual man?
A man who likes girls as well as the next fella.

What do you call this? (Stick out your tongue.)
   A lesbian with a hard-on!

* * *

Did you hear about the two Irish gays?
   Patrick Fitzhenry and Henry Fitzpatrick.

* * *

What do you call a faggot in a wheelchair?
   Rollaids!

* * *

Why didn't the little Greek boy want to leave home?
   He didn't want to leave his brother's behind!

* * *

Why did the little Greek boy finally leave home?
   He wasn't being reared properly!

* * *

Did you hear about the new gay bar?
   It's called Boys-R-Us.

* * *

What's the definition of a lesbian?
   Just another damn woman trying to do a man's job.

* * *

What's the definition of confusion?
   Twenty blind lesbians in a fish market.

* * *

Did you hear about the new breakfast cereal called Queerios?
   Add milk and they eat themselves.

Why was the queer fired from the sperm bank?
  He was caught drinking on the job.

* * *

What was Billy Jean King's latest advertising sponsor?
  Snap-on tools of America!

* * *

When a man and woman get married, they need a marriage license. What do lesbians need?
  A licker license.

* * *

Did you hear about the new Chinese restaurant for gays?
  It's called Sum Yung Gai!

* * *

Hear about the new disease gay musicians are coming down with?
  Bandaids.

* * *

What do you call a gay dentist?
  A tooth fairy.

* * *

Did you hear that Ben Hur had a sex change?
  Now he's Ben Gay.

* * *

What's the definition of "thorny"?
  A thailor at thea.

What's a Greek gentleman?

A man who takes a girl out at least three times before he propositions her brother.

* * *

What's the difference between a priest and a homosexual?

The way they pronounce a-men.

* * *

Did you hear the one about the queer deaf-mute?

Neither did he.

* * *

This gay guy comes home and sees his roommate jerking off into a rubber. "What are you doing?"

"Just packing your lunch!"

* * *

A guy walks into a gay bar and says, "I'm thirsty." The bartender says, "Sit in a corner and be quiet." "I'm so thirsty, I could lick the sweat off a bull's balls!" complains the guy. "Mooooo!" says his neighbor.

* * *

Do you know the difference between a cock-sucker and a bacon, lettuce and tomato sandwich?

Have lunch with me!

* * *

There was a robbery in Greenwich Village today, and a detective chased the robber and shot and killed him. The thief was lying in the street dead, and there was a crowd standing there looking on. A gay man walked past and said, "What's going on here? Why is there a dead man in the street?" Another man said, "Well, this guy got killed by a dick." And the gay man said, "Well, what a way to go!"

Italian Jokes

What's the definition of a maniac?
   An Italian in a whorehouse with a credit card!

* * *

Did you hear that Alitalia and El Al were merging to form a new airline?
   It's going to be called Well I'll Tel Ya.

* * *

What's an innuendo?
   An Italian suppository.

* * *

Why is Italy shaped like a boot?
   Because they couldn't fit all that shit into a sneaker.

What's the definition of a cad?

An Italian who doesn't tell his wife he's sterile until after she's gotten pregnant.

* * *

How do you kill an Italian?

Smash the toilet seat down on his head while he's getting a drink.

* * *

How can you recognize an Italian airline?

The planes have hair under the wings.

* * *

What is the Italian national bird?

A fly!

* * *

These two Italians went fishing, and they found a really great spot and caught a lot of fish. One Italian told the other to mark the spot so they could be sure to come back to the same place. As they were leaving, Alfredo asked Pietro if he had marked the side of boat. "No," said Pietro. "What if we didn't get the same boat again?"

Jewish Jokes

Did you hear about the train robbery in Israel?

They got $20,000 in cash, and $20 million in pledges. The pledges were anonymous!

* * *

A man walks into a bar and sees a beautiful woman sitting at the end of it. She is so beautiful he cannot take his mind off her, so he calls the bartender over and says, "Take that woman a drink on me." The bartender says, "It won't work." "What do you mean, it won't work?" "That woman," says the barkeep, "is a hard-hearted bitch. You won't get nowhere with her — nobody does!" "Okay," says the guy. "How about this: you got any Spanish fly?" "Spanish fly? No," says the bartender, "I've got Jewish fly." "So, what the hell is Jewish fly?" "I don't know; I've never used it. You want to give it a try?" "Yes," says the guy, and the next chance he gets, on his way to the men's room, he reaches behind her back and drops the stuff in the woman's drink.

Nothing happens for a long time, but then all of a sudden he feels her body close against his, and her voice is whispering hotly in his ear, and she's saying, "I can't stand it anymore! You excite me so much ... take me shopping!"

* * *

What's the difference between a Jewish-American Princess and spaghetti?
Spaghetti wiggles when you eat it.

* * *

What's the Jewish dilemma?
Pork on sale!

* * *

There's a new chain of Japanese-Jewish restaurants. They're called Sosume!

* * *

What's a Jewish piano?
A cash register!

* * *

This old Jewish lady was on a bus talking to the passenger beside her and said, "I have good news and bad news."
The passenger said, "Tell me the bad news."
The woman said, "My son is gay."
The passenger said, "Well, what's the good news?"
And she replied, "He married a doctor!"

Why are synagogues round?

So the Jews can't run and hide in the corners when the collection basket is passed around.

* * *

Why won't a cobra bite a Jewish-American Princess?

Professional courtesy.

* * *

Why are Jewish men circumcised?

Jewish women won't buy anything unless it's 20 percent off.

* * *

Why don't Jewish-American Princesses like orgies?

Too many thank-you notes to write.

* * *

These two old, retired Jewish businessmen are sitting around in New York City, getting a little bored. They're discussing their future, deciding what to do, and one of them suggests, "Why don't we go to Florida?" The other says, "Well, maybe we shouldn't both go, but why doesn't *one* of us go?" And his friend says, "Well, why not you?" And the other one says okay, and he goes to Florida. He comes back a couple of weeks later, and his friend asks, "How was it?" And the guy says, "It was great! I ate, I drank, I met beautiful women — it was terrific!" His friend says, "You met beautiful women?" He says, "Yes! I met this incredible woman, and we went back to her room, and she started to undress. Then she undressed me, and before I knew it we were both naked! Then we were lying down on the bed, and she starts to rub cream cheese all over me, and then she rubs cream cheese on my penis! Then she puts a bagel on my penis and puts a piece of lox on top, and would you believe, she proceeds to eat it? It was terrific!" Well, the other is so excited, he decides to go to Florida himself. He goes and then comes back a couple of days later. He goes to see his friend, and he has a big frown on his face. The guy asks him, "What's wrong? Did you go where I said?" The guy says yes. "Well, did you meet the girl I told you about?" "Yes." "Did you go into her room?" "Yes." "Well, did she put the cream cheese on you?" "Yes." "And the bagel? And the lox?" "Yes." "Well, what's wrong?" "It looked so good, I ate it myself!"

Mexican Jokes

What do you get when you cross a Mexican and a Vietnamese?
A car thief who can't drive!

* * *

Did you hear about the Mexican fireman who had two sons?
He named the first one Jose and the second one Josb!

* * *

What did the Mexican do with his first 50¢ piece?
Married her.

* * *

Why do Mexican cars have such small steering wheels?
So they can drive with handcuffs on.

Why did the Mexicans want to win the battle of the Alamo so much?
Because they wanted a wall to write on!

* * *

Have you heard about the new Mexican disaster movie?
It's called *Tacolipsnow*!

* * *

Why don't Mexicans barbecue?
Because the beans slip through the grill!

* * *

Why do Mexicans drive low riders?
So they can cruise and pick lettuce at the same time.

* * *

Why do Mexicans eat refried beans?
Ever seen a Mexican that didn't fuck things up the first time around?

* * *

What do you get when you cross a Mexican and an octopus?
I don't know, but it sure can pick tomatoes.

* * *

What do you call a Mexican baptism?
Bean dip!

* * *

Why did they have to cancel drivers' education and sex education in Mexico?
The donkeys couldn't handle it.

How come the Mexican Army used only six hundred soldiers at the Alamo?

They only had two cars.

* * *

Why are scientists breeding Mexicans instead of rats for experiments?

They multiply faster, and you don't get as attached to them.

Polish Jokes

Did you know that a number of people in my family were seafaring and from Poland?

One of my cousins died on a sailing trip with other members of my family, and seven of my cousins died while digging his grave.

* * *

My family had the first two Polish astronauts in space. One of them went out for a space walk and came back and knocked on the spaceship door. The other astronaut said, "Who is it?"

* * *

What did the Polack give his wife on their wedding night that was long and hard?

His last name!

What do you get when you cross a Polack and a mongoloid with one leg?

A Polaroid one-step!

* * *

How do you get three Polacks off a couch?

Jerk one off, and the other two will come!

* * *

What do you call this? (Puff out your cheeks.)

Polish sperm bank!

* * *

A Polack goes into a deserted bar for a drink and there, seated at the last stool, is a huge gorilla having a drink. Amazed, the Polack calls the bartender over and asks him how he can allow a gorilla in his bar.

"Oh, that's nothing," says the bartender. "Watch this!" The bartender then goes to the end of the bar, reaches under the counter, pulls out a huge club and smashes the gorilla over the head as hard as he can. The gorilla reacts by jumping up on the bar and running around to the bartender and giving him a blow-job.

"Pretty amazing, huh," says the bartender, crossing back to the Polack as the gorilla crawls back onto the chair. "Yeah," agrees the Polack, "that's really something." "You want to try it?" asks the bartender with a glint in his eye. "Well, all right ... only don't hit me as hard as you hit the gorilla, okay?"

* * *

Do you know why Polacks bury their dead asses-up?

Because they need someplace to park their bicycles!

* * *

What do you get when you cross a Polack and a monkey?
    Nothing. A monkey's too smart to screw a Polack.

* * *

What did the Polack do before going to the cockfight?
    Greased his zipper!

* * *

Why did the Polack wrap his hamster in electrical tape?
    So it wouldn't explode when he screwed it.

* * *

How do you recognize a Polish pirate?
    He's wearing two eye patches!

* * *

What's the most useless thing on a Polish woman's body?
    A Polish man.

* * *

How do you recognize a Polish word processor?
    She's the one with Whiteout all over her computer screen.

* * *

Did you hear about the overnight millionaire?
    He went over to Poland with a hundred cases of Cheerios and sold them as bagel seeds.

What's a Polish cocktail?
  Perrier and water!

* * *

Why don't Polacks eat M&M's?
  They have a hard time peeling them!

* * *

What happens when a Pole doesn't pay his garbage bill?
  They don't deliver anymore.

* * *

How do you get an armed Polack out of a tree?
  Wave to him!

* * *

Why are there no gynecologists in Poland?
  Because they can't read lips.

* * *

Did you hear about the Polish firing squad?
  They stand in a circle.

* * *

Do you know why there are so few Polish suicides?
  Because it's hard to kill yourself jumping out a basement window.

Miscellaneous Jokes

Why can't they teach driver's education and sex education at the same time in Libya?
    It's too hard on the camel.

* * *

How many Russians does it take to change a light bulb?
    None! They already glow in the dark.

* * *

How do you say "69" in Chinese?
    Two can chew!

* * *

What's the difference between heaven and hell?
    In heaven the French are the cooks, the Germans are the mechanics, the British are the police, the Italians are the lovers, and the Swiss are the bankers.

In hell the French are the mechanics, the Germans are the police, the British are the cooks, the Italians are the bankers, and the Swiss are the lovers.

* * *

Do you know how you get one hundred Frenchmen into Le Car?
La Machine!

* * *

Do you know why the British ships came back from the Falkland Islands full of sheep?
War brides.

* * *

Why can't you circumcise Iranians?
There's no end to those pricks!

* * *

What do you get when you cross a Japanese lady and a Chinese lady?
A broad that sucks laundry.

* * *

What's an Irish seven-course meal?
A six-pack and a boiled potato!

* * *

What's Scotland?
A place where men are men, and sheep are nervous!

* * *

What do you call a Filipino contortionist?
A Manila folder!

Why don't Puerto Ricans like blow-jobs?
They're afraid they'll interfere with their unemployment benefits.

* * *

What do Orientals use dental floss for?
Blindfolds.

* * *

Why were all the Greek sailors wearing black armbands?
Because of a ship that went down with a thousand cases of Vaseline aboard!

Part Five
VERY SICK JOKES

"Mommy, Mommy, I can't lick the bowl!"
"Shut up or I'll flush!"

* * *

What do you call a woman in a china closet with no arms or legs?
   Crystal!

* * *

What do you call a man on the wall with no arms or legs?
   Art!

* * *

What do you call a woman with no arms or legs, hanging from the ceiling?
   Tiffany!

What do you call a man with no arms or legs in a swimming pool?
  Bob!

* * *

What do you call a man in front of your door with no arms or legs?
  Matt!

* * *

What do you call a man with no arms, legs, head or torso?
  Dick!

* * *

What goes "Mark! Mark!"?
  A dog with a harelip.

* * *

What goes "Mort! Mort!"?
  A bull with a cleft palate.

* * *

Why do women rub their eyes when they get out of bed in the morning?
  Because they don't have balls to scratch.

* * *

How can you tell if a woman is wearing panty hose?
  If her ankles swell up, she farts.

* * *

What is the last thing that goes through a bug's mind before hitting the windshield at 80 mph?
  Its asshole.

What do you do when you come across an elephant?
  Wipe if off!

* * *

What did Helen Keller consider oral sex?
  A manicure

* * *

What do you have when there are one hundred rabbits standing in a row and they are all hopping backward?
  A receding hareline.

* * *

Why do lions in Africa go around licking each other's rear ends?
  To get the taste of blacks out of their mouths.

* * *

What do a rooster and a lawyer have in common?
  A rooster clucks defiance.

* * *

Why did God create vacations?
  So he could get some really big sins.

* * *

What's green and hops from bed to bed?
  A prostitoad.

* * *

How long is hare on a rabbit?
  About ten seconds.

* * *

How do you stop an elephant from charging?
  Take away his credit cards.

What do you call two morons drinking a soft drink, eating an apple and singing?

The Moron, TAB, and Apple Choir.

* * *

Do you know when a Cub Scout becomes a Boy Scout?

When he eats a brownie!

* * *

I once knew a girl who was so thin, she had to walk by me twice to cast a shadow!

* * *

A bathroom graffito:

If you voted for Reagan, you can't shit here.

You left your asshole in Washington!

* * *

When he was born, something terrible happened. He lived!

* * *

He's high-strung ... but not high enough!

* * *

The staff threw him a big dinner. Unfortunately, it didn't hit him!

* * *

She'll go out with every Tom, Dick and Harry ... providing they bring Jack along!

* * *

He's the knife of the party!

I'm a product of a misspent youth — which I'm still misspending!

* * *

A word to the weird is sufficient!

* * *

"It's certainly nice to have someone like you with us this evening," said the nightclub comic to the annoying ringside heckler, "and may I be the first to shake you by the THROAT!"

* * *

"This may be a phallic symbol, but, gentlemen, it is also a cigar!"

* * *

Support mental health or it will kill you!

* * *

I'm a sadist, and my wife's a hypochondriac. All day I tell her how well she looks!

* * *

There's a fine line between genius and insanity — he's managed to erase that line!

* * *

It's okay to have problems ... but he's a Freudian smorgasbord!

* * *

My wife is an unindexed handbook on "How To Be Neurotic About Practically Everything"!

He's like the shy guy who showed up at analysis with a specimen bottle!

* * *

Then there's the psychiatrist who ushered out his last patient for the day, heaved a weary sigh of relief, locked his desk, turned on his hearing aid and went home!

* * *

The psychiatrist was candid. He turned to the mother and said, "This eccentricity in your daughter, couldn't that be termed hereditary?"

The mother was indignant. "I'll have you know, Doctor, there has *never* been any hereditary in our family!"

* * *

I felt great when I realized that my inferiority complex is bigger than anyone else's!

* * *

He never lets a day go by without doing someone good!

* * *

There's all kinds of prejudice going on. Take poverty. How come only poor people have it?!

* * *

I'd like to box your ears ... but would they sell?!

* * *

Her hat had so many flowers that three funerals followed her home!

She dresses like an unmade bed!

* * *

Is that your necktie, or is your hair showing through your T-shirt?

* * *

You know what a shift is?
A maternity dress for virgins!

* * *

This man was so mean, he went to the home of the blind with a hammer and flattened out the braille!

* * *

"My wife tried to poison our unborn child's mind against me. She wrote nasty little notes about me and swallowed them!"

* * *

I've stuck it out about as long as I can. Yes, and just about as often too!

* * *

I believe a little incompatibility is the spice of life.... Particularly if he has income and she is palatable!

* * *

What's the definition of a gossip?
Someone who puts one and one together — even if they're not!

* * *

His wife's so suspicious, if she finds no black or blonde hair on his jacket, she accuses him of running around with bald women!

She named her kids Bulova, Timex, Pulsar and Elgin — because they came like clockwork!

* * *

Tests proved that cigarettes gave mice cancer — so they passed a law to make it illegal to sell cigarettes to mice!

* * *

They now have queen-size cigarettes — same length as king-size, only they have a bigger butt!

* * *

A guy is walking on the beach one day and finds an old lantern buried in the sand. So he picks up the lantern and rubs it, and a genie pops out! And the genie says, "I will grant you one wish. What'll it be?" And the guy thinks and thinks, and finally says, "I wish my dick was long enough to touch the ground." "You got it," said the genie, and cut his legs off!

* * *

This guy goes to his doctor, and the doctor says, "Sit down. I have good news and bad news for you, and I'll tell you the good news first." The guy says, "What's that?" The doctor says, "Well, I examined all your data and found you had only twenty-four hours to live." And the guy goes, "Holy shit! That's the GOOD news? What's the bad news?" The doctor says, "Well, I should have called you yesterday!"

* * *

What do you have when you have two little green balls in your hand?
Kermit's undivided attention!

Did you hear about the guy in the water-skiing accident who lost both his legs? He wanted to sue, but couldn't. His lawyer told him he didn't have a leg to stand on!

* * *

This husband and wife are driving in a game preserve in Africa and run over a skunk. The husband says to the wife, "Hurry up, let's get this skunk and hide it — here comes the game warden!" The woman says, "Well, where do you want me to hide it?" And the man says, "Put it under your skirt." And the woman says, "But it stinks!" And the guy says, "Well, I got used to it. You ought to be used to it too!"

JOHN BALL
AUTHOR OF **IN THE HEAT OF THE NIGHT** INTRODUCING, **POLICE CHIEF JACK TALLON** IN THESE EXCITING, FAST-PACED MYSTERIES.

WAYNE D. OVERHOLSER

WESTERNS

FREE!!
BOOKS BY MAIL
CATALOGUE

BOOKS BY MAIL will share with you our current bestselling books as well as hard to find specialty titles in areas that will match your interests. You will be updated on what's new in books at no cost to you. Just fill in the coupon below and discover the convenience of having books delivered to your home.

PLEASE ADD $1.00 TO COVER THE COST OF POSTAGE & HANDLING.

- -

BOOKS BY MAIL

320 Steelcase Road E.,
Markham, Ontario L3R 2M1

210 5th Ave., 7th Floor
New York, N.Y., 10010

Please send Books By Mail catalogue to:

Name _____
(please print)

Address _____

City _____

Prov./State _____ P.C./Zip _____
(BBM1)